Prentice Hall Regents

Animal Watch

PRENTICE HALL REGENTS

A VIACOM COMPANY

Getting Ready to Read

Look at the pictures. Name some animals that make good pets. Tell what you would do to care for them.

dog	cat	rabbit	duck	pet
puppy	kitten	chicken	wash	feed
pony	fish	hamster	brush	clean

PET SHOW

VETERINARIAN

Look at each picture and read each sentence.
Then make up an ending to the story.

Losing Leo

by Cass Hollander

Monday, April 9

Dear Diary,

Leo's gone. We were coming back from Grandpa's house yesterday. We stopped for gas, and Leo jumped out of the car and ran away... lickety split! I don't know why. Maybe he was just tired of being in the car. I called him. We looked all over for him. We stayed there until it got dark. But Leo didn't come back and we had to leave without him.

It's raining. Leo hates to get wet. I hope it's not raining where he is. I hope that Leo is all right.

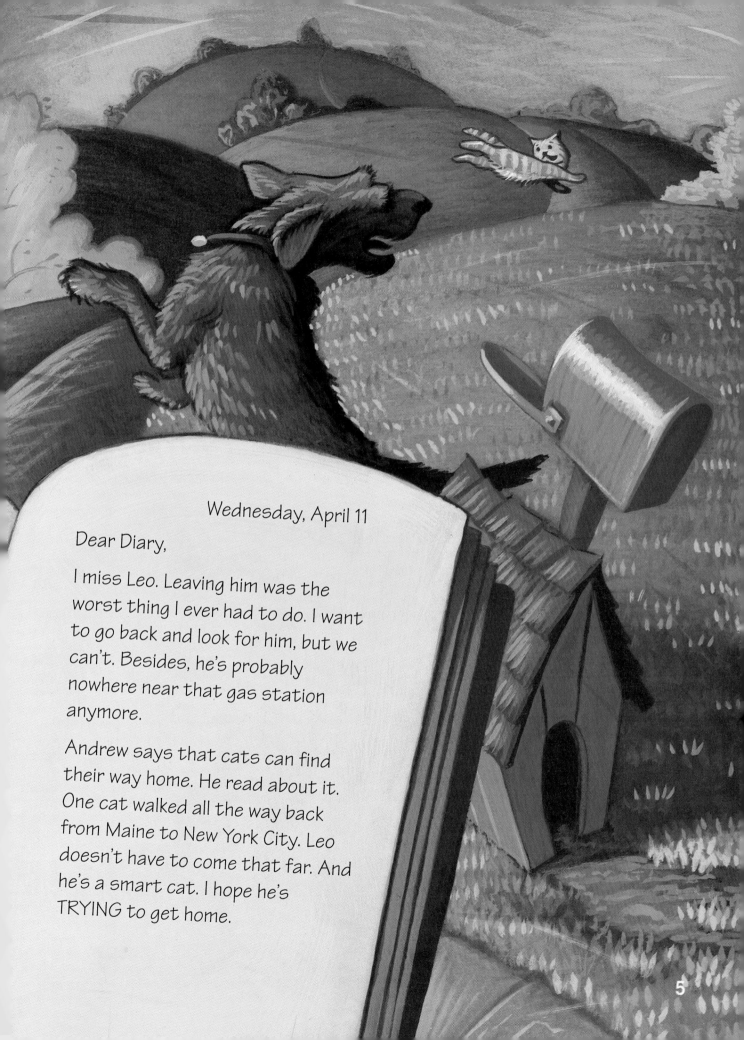

Wednesday, April 11

Dear Diary,

I miss Leo. Leaving him was the worst thing I ever had to do. I want to go back and look for him, but we can't. Besides, he's probably nowhere near that gas station anymore.

Andrew says that cats can find their way home. He read about it. One cat walked all the way back from Maine to New York City. Leo doesn't have to come that far. And he's a smart cat. I hope he's TRYING to get home.

Saturday, April 15

Dear Diary,

I watched a movie last night about two dogs and a cat who found their way home. They had to go over the mountains. It seemed to take them forever. The cat almost drowned. One of the dogs fell into a big hole and couldn't get out. But they made it. It was such a great movie. But it made me miss Leo even more.

I hope Leo's trying to get home. I hope he doesn't fall in any big holes. I miss him so much.

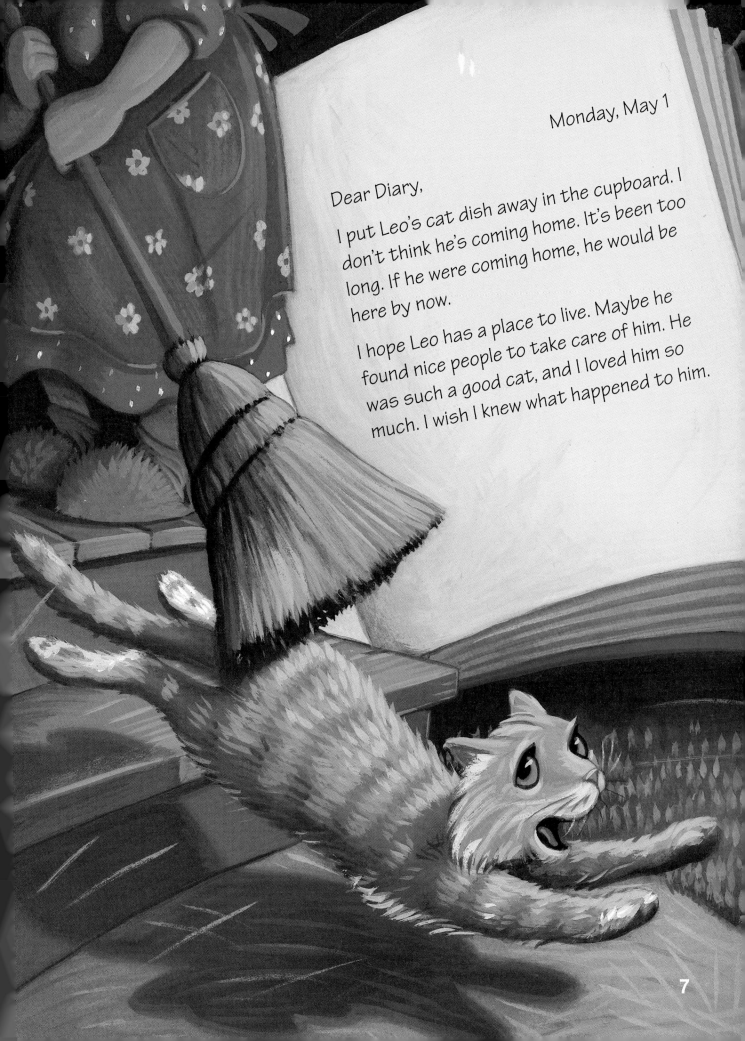

Monday, May 1

Dear Diary,

I put Leo's cat dish away in the cupboard. I don't think he's coming home. It's been too long. If he were coming home, he would be here by now.

I hope Leo has a place to live. Maybe he found nice people to take care of him. He was such a good cat, and I loved him so much. I wish I knew what happened to him.

Saturday, May 6

Dear Diary,
LEO'S BACK! He made it!

Here is a calendar that shows April 9 through May 6, the time that Leo was missing.

APRIL

Sunday	Monday	Tuesday	Wednesday	Thursday	Friday	Saturday
		1	2	3	4	5
6	7	8	9	10	11	12
13	14	15	16	17	18	19
20	21	22	23	24	25	26
27	28	29	30			

MAY

Sunday	Monday	Tuesday	Wednesday	Thursday	Friday	Saturday
				1	2	3
4	5	6	7	8	9	10
11	12	13	14	15	16	17

On a separate sheet of paper, write what you think Leo did each day he was gone. Look back at the story to help you. Remember: Leo must reach home on May 6.

LITERATURE
PART
2
NONFICTION

Animals by Day and Night

wild animal	elephant	hyena	beaver
habitat	lion	crocodile	mountain goat
plain	zebra	bear	sea otter

wolf	giraffe	sleep	hunt	lie down
pup	gorilla	float	care for	stand up
cub	den	fly	curl up	wake up

ANIMALS DON'T WEAR PAJAMAS
A BOOK ABOUT SLEEPING
BY EVE B. FELDMAN

Animals don't wear pajamas, and they don't have ticking clocks to tell them when it's time to go to sleep. But animals do know when it's time to rest.

When darkness falls, it's time for hummingbirds to sleep. They need lots of rest after a full day of darting forwards, backwards, and sideways. During the day these tiny birds flap their wings so fast that the wings seem to disappear. All night long they sit perfectly still in a deep sleep. They won't move again until sunrise.

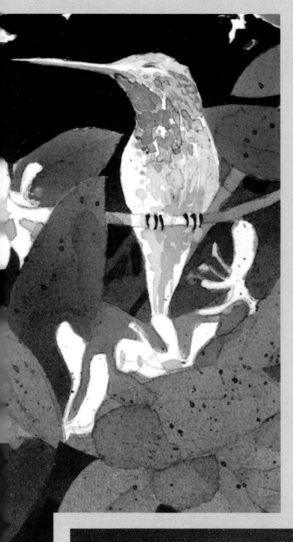

At night elephants lie down on their sides and go to sleep. They often snore. But after only two or three hours, their big, bulging bodies are no longer comfortable on the ground. So they wake up and rock themselves back and forth until they are on their feet again. If they are still tired, the elephants will have to finish their sleep standing up.

Lions sleep both day and night. Male lions usually sleep alone, and they may sleep as much as twenty-two out of twenty-four hours! Female lions spend most of their time with cubs and other females. They sleep less because it is their responsibility to hunt for food and care for the cubs.

Sea otters sleep floating in the water after wrapping themselves in strands of seaweed. These seaweed ties keep the otters from drifting away with the sway of the sea.

When a gray wolf is a new father, he will curl up to sleep outside his family's den. He guards his newborn pups and their mother who sleep inside.

Animals don't wear pajamas. But animals, just like people, do have their own special ways to sleep.

Who Am I?

Match each riddle to an animal picture.

I go to sleep lying down. After a few hours, I get uncomfortable, so I sleep standing up. Who am I?

I wrap myself in seaweed so I can float when I sleep. Who am I?

I sleep in a den with my pups. Who am I?

I sleep up to twenty–two hours a day. Who am I?

I stay perfectly still when I sleep. Who am I?

I wear pajamas and sleep in a bed. Who am I?

Animal News Bits

Python Visits Shore Family

Juan and Rita Ortiz had an unexpected visitor to their shore home this weekend—an 8-foot Southern Asian python! The family's 6-month-old dog, Cuco, discovered the snake under the front porch and would not stop barking until Juan came to check on it. Rita Ortiz grabbed a flashlight and ran to help her husband when she heard him yelling, "Rita, there's a really big snake under here!"

"I don't really mind snakes, so I thought this wouldn't be any big deal," said Rita Ortiz. "Boy, was I wrong!"

The snake was taken to the animal shelter by Wildlife Removers of Deal, New Jersey. Anyone who is missing a pet python should call 555-2211 for information.

LOST CAT

Black w/one white paw and bright gray eyes. Sad child waiting for your call. REWARD! 555-1626

FOUND

West Side, Parakeet, green and yellow. Sings "Happy Birthday." Please call 555-1816 soon or my kids will keep it!

Pet Classified Ads

Read the ads. How could you help find these lost pets?

LOST SHEEPDOG

Female. Long, gray hair, blue collar, answers to "Snickers." Last seen near Riverview Shopping Mall. Call Tom at 555-4780.

LOST DOG

8-year-old Collie, tan w/red collar. Answers to Muffy. Freeport area 555-2759

Strange but True Animal Facts

Bats Use Radar!

Bats are the only mammals that can fly. These small, furry, winged animals are nocturnal, hunting at night and sleeping in the daytime. Bats have good eyesight (the saying "blind as a bat" isn't true) but to find insects in the dark, they need to use other senses, too. They send out ultrasonic waves—sounds that are too high for people to hear. More than one hundred sound waves each second pulse out from the bats' noses or mouths. The waves bounce off objects, and the bats' big ears catch the echoes. The bats can tell where an object is, how big it is, and how fast and in what direction it is going. This way of finding objects by using sound waves is called echolocation. Airplane pilots use echolocation or radar to land their planes.

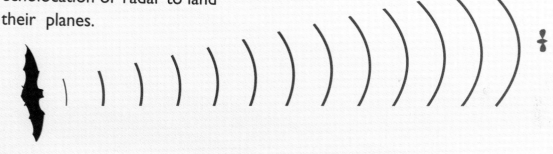

Cat and Dog Riddles

What do you get when you cross a dog with a clock?

watch dog

What does a cat rest its head on when it goes to sleep?

cat-er-pillow

What kind of shoes do mice wear to get away from cats?

squeakers

How can you tell you have a slow dog?

It brings you yesterday's paper.

Why does a cat have a fur coat?

Because he would look silly in a raincoat!

19

EVERYDAY TALK

- Inviting someone to do something
- Accepting or turning down an invitation

Here are other ways to invite someone:

> How about coming to my house?
> Can you come over on Saturday?
> Do you want to come to my house on Saturday?

You can accept an invitation or turn it down.

Accept:
Okay!
Thanks, I'd love to.
Yes, that would be great!

Turn Down:
Thanks, but I'm busy.
Sorry, I wish I could.

Work with a partner. Act out this situation:
Partner 1: Invite your friend to go somewhere with you.
Partner 2: Accept or turn down the invitation.

HERE AND THERE

All over the world, there are animals that live and work with people. Some are used for transportation, carrying people and goods. Other animals help people hunt or work. Some animals give milk that people drink. And some animals are sacred to the people they live among.

Desert camel caravan

Woman with guide dog

Coal miner with canary

Police with bloodhound

Do you know other ways that animals help people? Tell about them.

Horses on cattle ranches

Theme Project

It's almost time to open up the Zoo! What do you have to do before opening day? Find out by answering these questions.

1. Do we have enough animals in our Zoo?

2. Does our Zoo protect the animals and people from one another?

3. Have we made the right homes for all our animals? Will all of them be able to sleep well?

4. Have we included things to make people comfortable, such as benches, snack bars, rest rooms, and water fountains?

5. Are there enough signs and maps to direct people?

EXIT

REST ROOMS

First Aid

6. How can we tell people that our Zoo is ready to open?

Zoo Map

Lions Den

COME TO THE ZOO

ZOO OPENS SOON!

Theme Game
Animal Wheel

Play Animal Wheel. Roll one to four dice and find the animal for that number. If you can name the animal, your team gets one point. The team with the most points wins.

Prentice Hall Regents
Publisher: Marilyn Lindgren
Project Editors: Carol Callahan, Kathleen Ossip
Assistant Editor: Susan Frankle
Director of Production: Aliza Greenblatt
Manufacturing Buyer: Dave Dickey
Production Coordinator: Ken Liao
Marketing Manager: Richard Seltzer

McClanahan & Company, Inc.
Editorial, Design, Production and Packaging
Project Director: Susan Cornell Poskanzer
Creative Director: Lisa Olsson
Design Director: Toby Carson
Director of Production: Karen Pekarne

© 1996 by Prentice Hall Regents
Prentice Hall, Inc.
A Viacom Company
Upper Saddle River, NJ 07458

PRENTICE HALL REGENTS
A VIACOM COMPANY

Printed in the United States of America

10 9 8 7 6 5 4 3 2

ISBN 0-13-349846-8

Prentice-Hall International (UK) Limited, London
Prentice-Hall of Australia Pty. Limited, Sydney
Prentice-Hall Canada Inc., Toronto
Prentice-Hall Hispanoamerican, SA., Mexico
Prentice-Hall of India Private Limited, New Delhi
Prentice-Hall of Japan, Inc., Tokyo
Simon & Schuster Asia Pte. Ltd., Singapore
Editora Prentice-Hall do Brasil, Ltda., Rio de Janeiro

Acknowledgments
Grateful acknowledgment is made to the following publishers, authors, and agents for their permission to reprint copyrighted material. The following literature appears in both Teacher's and Student Books:

Henry Holt and Company: From *Animals Don't Wear Pajamas: A Book About Sleeping.* Text by Eve B. Feldman, illustrated by Mary Beth Owens. Text copyright © 1992 by Eve B. Feldman. Illustrations copyright © 1992 by Mary Beth Owens. Reprinted by permission of Henry Holt and Co.

Cover
Carlos Ochagaria

Photography
Lisa Donovan p18 (bottom); J.H. Robinson/Animals, Animals p18 (top); Ken Karp Photography p22

Illustration
Meg Aubrey p21; Daniel Del Valle p19 (top right, bottom); Linda Howard p22; Vinton Lennon p9; Paul Meinel p18–19; Ann Neumann p10–11, p17; Pronto Design p23; Ken Spengler p4–8; Ron Zalme p17, p20